MONSTER SCIENCE

THE SCIENCE BEHIND
VAMPIRES, WITCHES, AND GHOSTS

JOY LIN AND VIOLET TOBACCO

Gareth Stevens
PUBLISHING

Please visit our website,
www.garethstevens.com.
For a free color catalog of all
our high-quality books, call
toll free 1-800-542-2595 or
fax 1-877-542-2596.

Published in 2025 by
Gareth Stevens Publishing
2544 Clinton St.
Buffalo, NY 14224

First published in Great Britain in 2021 by Wayland
Text © Joy Lin, 2021
Artwork and design © Hodder and Stoughton, 2021

Editors: Elise Short and Grace Glendinning
Designer: Peter Scoulding
Illustration: Violet Tobacco

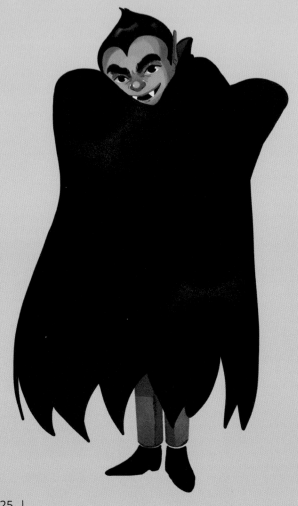

Cataloging-in-Publication Data

Names: Lin, Joy, author. | Tobacco, Violet, illustrator.
Title: The science behind vampires, witches, and ghosts /
  by Joy Lin, illustrated by Violet Tobacco.
Description: Buffalo, New York : Gareth Stevens Publishing, 2025. |
  Series: Monster science | Includes glossary and index.
Identifiers: ISBN 9781538294291 (pbk.) | ISBN 9781538294307 (library bound) |
  ISBN 9781538294314 (ebook)
Subjects: LCSH: Vampires--Juvenile literature. | Witches--Juvenile literature. |
  Ghosts--Juvenile literature. | Science--Juvenile literature.
Classification: LCC GR830.V3 L56 2025 | DDC 398.21--dc23

Printed in the United States of America

CPSIA compliance information: Batch #CSGS25: For further information contact Gareth Stevens at 1-800-542-2595.

Find us on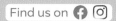

CONTENTS

INTRODUCTION

At night, in the dark, under your blankets, does the thought of a prowling vampire chill your blood? Do you worry about a witch casting a paralyzing spell on you? Are you aghast at the thought of a ghost hovering above your bed?

Then you've come to the right place. This book is here to set out the science behind these legendary monsters. You'll find out just how likely it is that: a) they are fact rather than fiction; b) they could do you any harm; and c) you could beat them with science.

Meet the Monsters

Let's start with vampires. According to legend, vampires are dead people who have come back to life and drink blood to sustain themselves. They are pale, have fangs, emerge at night, and avoid sunshine ... but where do these legends come from?

There are some interesting theories to explain vampires. One is a medical condition, called *cutaneous porphyrias*. Sufferers generally have very pale skin from avoiding daylight, because exposure to sunlight causes burning pain, redness, swelling, itching, and even blisters.

At a time when medical understanding was limited, this condition seemed mysterious and supernatural, especially since it's thought that a treatment at this time included drinking blood!

Avoiding sunlight, a pale complexion, drinking blood ... did these symptoms lead to the idea of an evil, bloodsucking creature that comes out at night?

What about witches? They appear in fiction in many different guises, from the beautiful lady with a magic wand who makes your dreams come true, to a green-skinned, wart-nosed, nasty old woman who flies on a broomstick and makes evil potions in her enormous cauldron.

Witches aren't always female, but they seem to have started out as real-life wise women, who claimed to cast spells and make healing potions. The evil side of things crept in during the 15th century in Europe, when awful, unexplained events occurred, such as storms, crop failures, diseases, and other natural disasters. Without the scientific knowledge we have to explain these events today, women accused of being witches often took the blame for whipping up these disasters.

What is fact and what is fiction when it comes to witches?

Now on to ghosts. When we think of ghosts, we tend to think of floaty, semitransparent versions of people who have died. They've come back to visit or haunt the living because of unfinished business. Stories of ghosts, spirits, phantoms, lost souls, and more exist in most cultures around the world and have done so since ancient times. But where does this idea come from?

In many cultures and religions, it is thought that when a person dies, their soul or spirit leaves their body and continues to exist. This is why people around the world have specific rituals, to make sure that the dead person's spirit won't come back to haunt them.

But so many places are said to be haunted; so many people claim to have seen, or sometimes *felt*, a ghost ... surely there must be some truth to the existence of the spirit world? Well, let's see what science has to say about that.

Mysteries can be frightening. Before science came along, people used their imaginations to provide explanations for anything odd that happened. Even today, lots of people are superstitious about the events of the world. Let's put these beliefs and superstitions to the test as we find out the truth behind vampires, witches, and ghosts.

Feeling brave? Then let's get started ...

Vampires

What do we know about vampires, and how would we recognize one? In films, folktales, stories, and on TV, the characteristics of vampires vary, but these are the main traits that unite them.

Vampires:
- look like pale humans with fangs
- sleep in coffins during the day and come out at night
- bite humans and drink their blood
- can turn into bats
- cast no reflections in the mirror and have no shadow
- don't like silver or garlic
- can be killed by sunlight, a stake through the heart, decapitation, or a combination of the above.

Simple! And with that list of very specific descriptions, you've got an idea of how to spot a vampire. But are vampires real? The stories must have come from somewhere ...

WHERE DID IT ALL BEGIN?

Apart from the *cutaneous porphyria* idea, there are other theories about vampires' origins. One is linked to how a body decomposes. Sometimes, a dead person looks rounder than they did in life. For a while, no one knew why, so they made up an explanation: the dead person was a vampire by night, filling itself up with blood! In truth, the body swells due to a buildup of gases produced during decomposition.

BLOODY LIPS

Another strange phenomenon that probably contributed to the belief in vampires is linked to the effect diseases, such as (the now treatable) tuberculosis and bubonic plague, had on dead bodies. These diseases would cause blood to accumulate in the lungs. As the corpse was handled, blood would come up through the throat to the mouth. Imagine seeing a corpse that's fatter than it was when it was alive ... *and* has blood on its lips! If you didn't know what was going on, you might leap to conclusions too!

HAIR-RAISING

Something else that probably influenced vampire tales is the idea that a corpse's hair and nails keep on growing, even though it's dead. The thing is, they aren't actually growing – it's all part of the decomposition process.

Here's what actually happens. After death, moisture evaporates from the skin. This makes the skin around the nail shrink, so more nail is revealed. It isn't new nail, it was already there. It's the same with hair. Lack of moisture means the scalp starts to waste away. So hair sticking out of the scalp looks like it's growing longer, when, in fact, it's the flesh that has shrunk to reveal hair that was already there!

ONCE BITTEN

Then there's a theory that links vampirism (acting like a vampire) with rabies. Rabies is a hideous disease that can be transmitted to humans via a bite from an infected animal, such as a dog or vampire bat. When infected with rabies, you can suffer from:
• extreme sensitivity to things affecting your senses, such as the brightness of sunlight and the strong smell of garlic
• difficulty sleeping, which can make you more active at night.

Sounds familiar, doesn't it?

In time, these traits made their way into folktales and scary stories, and eventually evolved into the vampire we know and fear today.

Let's Talk Fangs!

People might have believed in vampires in the past, but could a vampire survive in today's world? And could he hide from us successfully?

Let's look into a vampire's fangs. Fangs are the long, sharp teeth – sometimes called canines – that meat-eating animals, such as cats, dogs, spiders, and snakes, all have. These predators use their canine teeth to bite and hold their prey in place, and to tear into its flesh. Nasty!

Some snakes and spiders have fangs that are hollow with a hole at the tip, so they can also deliver a dose of venom to immobilize or kill their victim. It's a bit like having a shot when you're sick, except snake venom won't make you better.

So, what sort of fangs would this modern vampire have? Solid to create a wound they can drink from, or hollow to paralyze or poison its victim?

Folding Fangs

Most snakes' fangs are visible when they open their mouths, but our vampire's fangs should probably be more discreet. With fangs in full view whenever a vampire talked, they'd be far too obvious – and would make vampire hunters' work very easy.

But what if the vampire had a viper's teeth? The viper family has fangs on a hinge. The fangs are folded up against the roof of the viper's mouth, and only flick out when needed. Sounds like just the kind a monster would want – so let's assume we're facing poison-filled, drop-down fangs with our vampire.

CAUTION: POISON

Our vampire will have to be very careful with these sharp, poison-filled teeth in his mouth. He's probably not equipped with the natural defenses vipers are born with. So how *do* snakes keep from killing themselves with an accidental bite to the cheek?

The first thing to know is that the viper's poison is stored in specialized compartments, with only one exit: the fangs. Vipers have also developed an immunity to the poisonous chemicals. They produce proteins inside their bodies that bind and deactivate venom in the blood. Amazing stuff!

Our vampire would probably have quite a hard time evolving such complex systems before accidentally biting his tongue ...

BALANCED BLOODY DIET

The human body needs a balanced diet of protein, carbohydrates, and fat to stay healthy. So, if all vampires consume is blood, they'd have to drink a lot of it to get the nutrition they need to sustain themselves.

But here's the problem: blood is rich in iron, which can be rough on the digestive system. Human bodies only need a tiny amount of it. Too much iron can cause all sorts of unpleasant side effects, including dizziness, weight loss, and gray skin. (Hmm ... that last one definitely sounds like a vampire.)

So perhaps our vampire's body is doing something similar to vampire bats, whose only food source is blood. How do vampire bats cope with this huge amount of iron?

COMPLETELY BATTY!

To meet its energy needs, a vampire bat has to drink close to half its body weight in blood at each meal. Blood is made up of about 80 percent water, so within five minutes of drinking, the bat begins peeing out the extra liquid.

More importantly, vampire bats have a mucous membrane inside their intestines that acts as a barrier to prevent the absorption of too much iron. They also have lots of little blood vessels that work to absorb the good bits of blood more quickly than humans can.

So perhaps vampires are always peeing and have somehow evolved iron-blocking mucus membranes? Sounds messy!

The fact that vampire bats exist in real life could explain why, in some vampire stories, vampires can turn into bats. And not just one bat, but a whole colony!

Let's think about the logistics of splitting one living being into dozens of living beings. What would happen if one of the bats got lost or trapped, and wasn't able to rejoin the colony (in this case, our vampire)? Would the vampire end up missing a finger or some other body part? Quite a risky business!

Conservation of Bats

Apart from the risk of missing fingers, we also have to consider an important law of science called "conservation of mass," which says:

Matter (the stuff everything is made of) can't be created or destroyed; it can only be transformed.

So in any reaction or transformation, you should end up with exactly the same amount of matter you started with, because there's nowhere else for the matter to go. If our vampire weighs 200 pounds (90 kg) before turning into the colony of bats, the collective weight of the bats should still be 200 pounds (90 kg). A vampire bat only weighs 0.1 ounce (3 g), so that's about 30,000 bats in this colony! That's hundreds of times bigger than even the biggest bat colonies.

Mirror Mirror

Remember two other major characteristics of vampires: no reflection in mirrors and no shadow. Let's look at mirrors first.

In the past, pure silver was used to create mirrors. Vampires, of course, hate silver! This is probably where the legend about their reflections comes from. Silver also reflects ultraviolet (UV) rays of the sun, which vampires must avoid.

So, silver mirrors are a big no-no, but today's mirrors use materials that absorb most of the dangerous UV rays in sunshine, so maybe our vampire would be safe? Not necessarily. Lots of smooth surfaces reflect quite a bit of UV light – sand, snow, even a bowl of water.

According to legend, if there's any natural light involved, our vampire is in danger. This is good news for you, as it's very tricky to avoid all reflective surfaces!

Shadow Play

If our vampire and all his clothing magically cast no shadows, he would have to avoid *all* light sources – natural or unnatural, inside or outside – to avoid giving away his identity. Since shadows are created when light rays are blocked, it would be impossible to hide every time somebody flipped on a light. It's a dead giveaway.

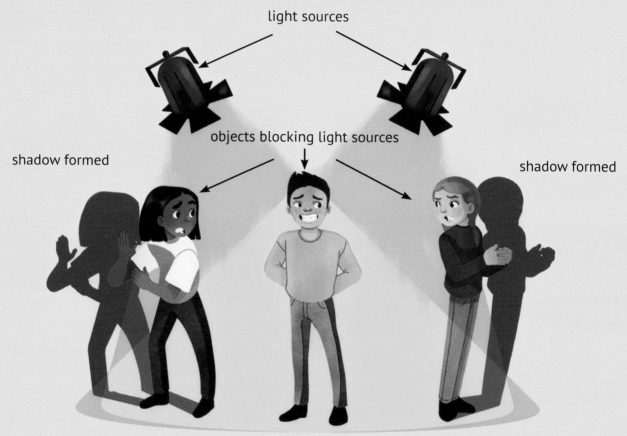

light sources

objects blocking light sources

shadow formed

shadow formed

no shadow – vampire!

Unfit for Modern Times

It seems highly unlikely that a vampire could live in today's world undetected. With the amount of blood a vampire would need to drink every day, the number of victims would have to be really high. With modern technology, including cell phones in everyone's hands, it would be difficult to keep up the bloodthirsty activities without ever getting caught on camera. Not to mention, a picture of our shadowless, reflection-less friend would surely be an instant viral sensation! Not great for keeping a low profile.

vampire sightings: IMPOSSIBLE!

Witches

When you think of a witch, do you imagine an old woman wearing a long, black dress and a pointy hat, with green skin and warts? Does she spend her days flying around on a broom, or stirring potions in a huge cauldron? She sounds pretty out-there, doesn't she?

Fact or Fiction?

So where do these descriptions come from, and has this sort of witch ever existed?

In the Shade

Let's start with the idea of green skin. Human skin comes in many different shades, depending on the presence of a pigment called melanin. Melanin is produced by cells in the skin called melanocytes. People with light skin mostly produce pheomelanin, which is red to yellow in color; people with dark skin mostly produce eumelanin, which varies from dark brown to black.

Melanin protects your skin, especially from the sun's harmful rays, though it doesn't stop you from burning. Of course, some skin tones can also turn red with heat and blue with cold, but any other color just isn't healthy. Let's look at a few worrisome shades.

Not-So-Mellow Yellow

If your skin and eyes turn a strong shade of yellow, you probably have jaundice. It isn't an illness in itself, but a symptom of certain illnesses that have caused a buildup of a pigment called bilirubin. Jaundice suggests the liver isn't working properly for some reason, as it's the liver's job to break down bilirubin and send it out in your poop.

Green is a more unusual skin color, but you might have noticed your skin can turn a light shade of green when it's bruised. Pale, greenish skin can also be a sign of anemia, which is caused by a lack of hemoglobin (a protein that transports oxygen in your blood) in the body. It causes tiredness and lack of energy, which doesn't sound very witchlike. Witches need to be alert to whiz around on broomsticks and brew their potions.

It's Not Easy Being Green

As it happens, the real reason we associate witches with green skin has nothing to do with science, and everything to do with Hollywood. In the original book *The Wonderful Wizard of Oz*, the Wicked Witch of the West wasn't even a little bit green.

However, when the MGM film studio adapted the story in 1939, when color films were new, the producers thought a green-skinned witch looked suitably evil. The color showed up so well on film that the association stuck.

In order to create the color, however, Margaret Hamilton, the actress playing the witch, had to be covered in a copper-based paint. Small amounts of copper are essential in a healthy human body, but excess copper is poisonous. If she'd swallowed any of the paint, it could have made her seriously ill, so the poor old Wicked Witch of the West was forced to suck up her meals through a straw!

WART'S THAT?

Another witchy skin condition is warts. When people were really panicking about witches back in the 1600s, warts were considered "the devil's mark." Some people even believed that a wart on a witch was like a nipple, or teat, which she used to feed her evil pets!

So what is a wart *really*?

Warts are small growths of extra cells under the skin, often caused by a virus. You don't have to be old to get warts, and having them certainly doesn't mean you're evil! However, centuries ago, when there wasn't much understanding of medical conditions, people with any sort of rare issue were treated with suspicion. It's safe to say that warts have nothing to do with witchcraft whatsoever!

FLYING A BROOMSTICK

How likely is it that a witch could fly on a broomstick? Well, it would definitely be uncomfortable.

Imagine riding a bike. Now take away the seat so you're riding on the frame (ouch!). On this rounded, narrow surface, your weight can't be distributed evenly, so balance would be tricky. You don't have any pedals, of course, so your dangling legs are just adding more weight and pressure. You'll soon get a numb bum. There aren't any handlebars either, so how would you steer it without tumbling off?

More importantly, how would you even get it off the ground?

Not ready for liftoff!

Up, Up, and Away

Think about how a helicopter takes to the sky. It rises straight up and hovers over the ground, its spinning blades creating an upward-pushing force, called lift, by pushing air downwards.

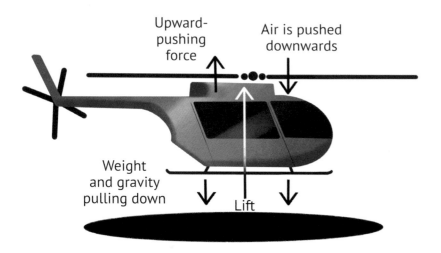

Upward-pushing force

Air is pushed downwards

Weight and gravity pulling down

Lift

This follows Newton's Third Law of Motion:

For every action, there is an equal and opposite reaction.

Once a helicopter is airborne, another rotor on its tail is used for steering. To go left, you'd push air to the right, just as you change directions when you're swimming (pushing the water). Smaller flying machines, such as jet packs, work the same way: by pushing downwards in order to move up.

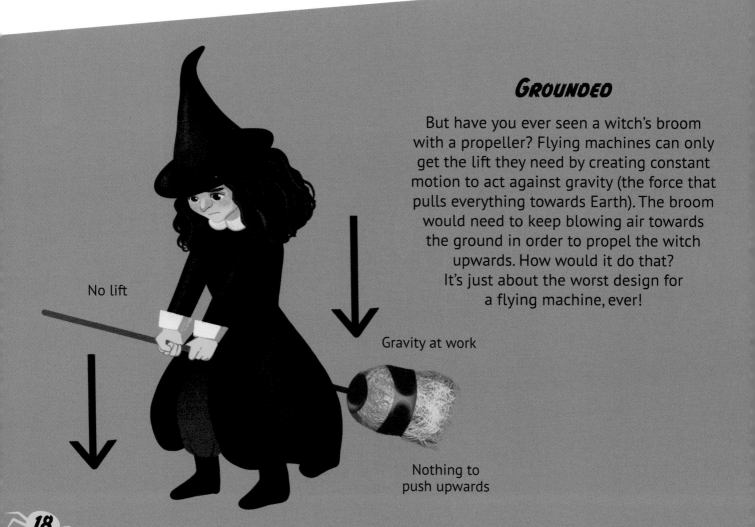

Grounded

But have you ever seen a witch's broom with a propeller? Flying machines can only get the lift they need by creating constant motion to act against gravity (the force that pulls everything towards Earth). The broom would need to keep blowing air towards the ground in order to propel the witch upwards. How would it do that? It's just about the worst design for a flying machine, ever!

No lift

Gravity at work

Nothing to push upwards

BREATHLESS

Let's say a witch could manage to stay on the broom without flipping upside down in the breeze. She'd have to deal with all the issues pilots suffered from in the first planes – lots of objects hitting her in the face, including rain, bugs, and birds!

She'd also need to find a way to stay warm, because the higher she flew, the colder it would get. This is because the higher you go, the lower the air pressure becomes. Air pressure is the pushing force of air molecules. The pressure decreases as you go higher because there are fewer molecules in the air. This affects the temperature, which also goes down. Another consequence of low pressure and fewer air molecules is that there is less oxygen, so breathing is very difficult.

The witch would have to wear goggles, an oxygen mask attached to an oxygen tank, and a big, fluffy sweater over her black dress. Doesn't look very frightening, does it? All in all, it seems highly unlikely a witch would ever get off the ground.

The dream

The reality

POTIONS!

Witches are also famous for using their knowledge of plants to make potions that heal … or harm. Could a person really use plants to make magic?

Well, some plants naturally make chemicals to protect themselves from predators and diseases. Some of these chemicals can cause serious harm to humans, including death or the "milder" side effect of vivid hallucinations. Some plants can have more positive effects, which have confused and amazed humans throughout history. It's not surprising that many plants have been considered magical through the centuries.

Sage, for example, was thought to have magical properties by the ancient Romans, and all the way through the Middle Ages. Sage is known to help repel insects and make the air more breathable for people with asthma. The smoke from burning sage can even be used to disinfect the air by clearing away bacteria.

Ginger improves digestion, and chamomile helps with sleep, colds, fevers, and stomach problems.

Science can now explain how the chemicals in both plants give them "healing powers":

Sage

Ginger

Chamomile

- Ginger increases the production of bile, a liquid produced by the liver that is important in digestion.

- Dried chamomile flowers contain chemicals that have a relaxing effect. Research into their effects shows they fight allergies, reduce swelling, protect cells, and guard against cancer.

St. John's wort contains active antidepressants, which are substances that can help reduce anxiety.

Milk thistle can be used to treat stomach pain because it contains a compound that protects the body's cells.

So maybe inside that mysterious, bubbling witch's cauldron there was just a concoction of herbal home remedies that people thought were magic rather than medicine.

POISONED?

Between the 15th and 17th centuries, people were terrified of witches – usually poor women who may have used herbs and other natural remedies – and witch hunts became common. The most famous witch hunt of all happened in the area of Salem in Massachusetts.

It all began when three young girls started behaving strangely. They had fits, screamed, and threw things. Weirdly, their behavior spread to other girls in the town. Witchcraft was suspected as no other explanation could be found, and they seemed to have been taken over by something evil. The witch hunt that followed resulted in the unfair trials and killing of many innocent women.

No one knows for sure what happened to the girls, but one theory says they ate a poisonous fungus growing on local rye plants. Once eaten, the fungus affects the human nervous system, causing victims to have fits and suffer hallucinations. If true, it would be another interesting example of the power found in nature.

SCAPEGOATS

People throughout history were afraid of witches because they just didn't know enough about science. Before microscopes were invented, no one knew microorganisms existed, so no one had a clue about germs. When people fell sick, they made up stories to explain it. Tales of curses and dark magic spread fast, and so-called witches became the scapegoats – women who were easy to blame when the truth wasn't so obvious.

They might not have had green faces or ridden broomsticks, and their warts weren't evil, but so-called witches were once very real. The good news is, many were just wise women who could heal you of various ailments, but were being accused of all sorts of things they hadn't done. So if you ever meet a witch like the ones misunderstood throughout history, there's probably no need to be afraid.
Why not ask her if she can teach you about plants?

warty WITCHES: NOT REAL!

Ghosts

The idea of haunting spirits exists in most cultures. These "ghosts" usually have similar origins: after someone dies, their spirit, with their memories from life, still lingers on. The descriptions of the ghosts themselves vary. Sometimes they're described as a semitransparent being, able to pass through walls. Some are said to be visible to humans, and some are invisible but can be felt, making those nearby feel cold.

GHOSTS VS. SCIENCE

The ideas we have about ghosts raise a lot of questions about the scientific and practical likeliness of their existence. So let's consider what being a ghost would really be like.

THE UNTOUCHABLES

When ghosts are shown in movies and described in books, one of the hardest things to understand is how they move around. Often, they are portrayed as intangible beings (meaning they cannot be touched). Other characters are able to walk straight through the ghosts as if they are wisps of light, instead of tangible (touchable) objects. On the other hand, those same ghosts are often decribed as walking on roads, climbing stairs, getting into elevators, or even driving cars.

How does that make sense? If your body cannot interact with your surroundings, then shouldn't that rule apply to every part of you, even your bum when sitting, or the soles of your feet on the pavement?

Not going anywhere

GOING NOWHERE

If you can pass through walls and people, then you can't stand on the floor. You would have to be floating all the time, because the act of walking requires interaction with the ground. Every step you take consists of your foot pushing down and back against the floor, propelling you up and forwards. Even moving through the air requires interaction with the air molecules, so intangible ghosts would be stuck in one place!
Filmmakers: pick a story and stick with it!

SEEING THROUGH YOU

Have you wondered why ghosts are often shown in films as translucent (semi-see-through) versions of their former selves?

In the late 18th century, "optical shows" featuring hazy projections of images in light became hugely popular because the technology was brand new and exciting. Imagine having never seen a film before, and suddenly glowing pictures floated in front of you! At the same time, in the art world, semitransparent watercolor was all the rage for painting scenes and portraits. A combination of these huge cultural trends led to writers, such as British author Charles Dickens (1812–70), depicting ghosts in their work as see-through, and the idea continues today.

FOGGY SOUL

Another theory for the hazy, white version of ghosts goes back to the Stone Age. It's thought that early humans saw their foggy breath on a cold day and believed it was their soul. They believed this soul kept them alive, because they saw it leave the body after people had been killed by animals.

At the time, people didn't know the science of condensation: that the heat of our body's breath condenses the nearby water molecules in the air, changing them from a gas to a liquid. It's just breath fog!

Buried Alive!

What about ghosts draped in white cloth or sheets?
Where on Earth did that idea come from?

Traditionally, the dead were buried in white shrouds, so a white sheet was the last piece of fabric a person was seen in. While this practice was widely used, not much was understood about a medical condition called catalepsy, which can make sufferers lose consciousness and become physically stiff. It can last for hours. Catalepsy sufferers would often be presumed dead, and would wake up days later, wrapped in a white shroud. They would then rise up, robed in white – perhaps in the middle of their own funeral service – and their mourners would have been terrified! They were actually quite lucky compared to some poor souls. At least they woke up before they were buried alive ...

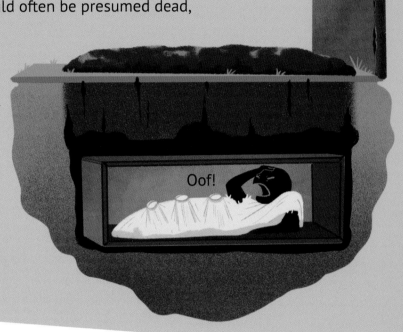

Oof!

Haunted House

But what about the stories of haunted houses, in which you can hear creaking noises or footsteps when no one but you is there? Where areas feel unnaturally chilly, and objects appear to move on their own? Can science explain these phenomena?

Different people have reported seeing, hearing, and feeling things in the exact same part of a supposedly haunted house, even though they've never met and discussed their stories. Were they all lying? Not necessarily. However, just because they believed what they saw doesn't mean they actually saw it.

25

QUESTIONABLE PIPEWORK

In the 1950s, a French scientist named Vladimir Gavreau discovered that when a pipe of a certain length and thickness vibrates near a person, it can cause anything from annoyance to serious pain, depending on how sensitive that person is to the frequency of the sound. However, not all vibrations make sound waves that our brains can interpret, though our ears can still sense them. That's what Gavreau discovered: infrasound is a noise that occurs at such a low frequency that we don't consciously notice it.

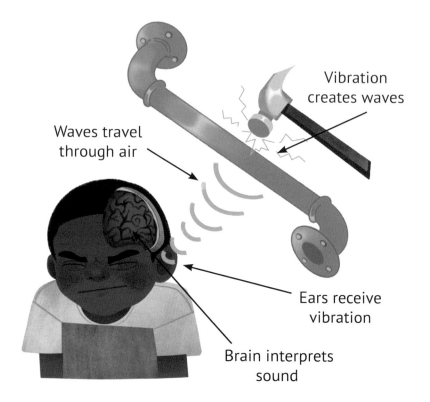

Vibration creates waves

Waves travel through air

Ears receive vibration

Brain interprets sound

BAD VIBRATIONS

Soundwaves are measured in a unit called hertz (Hz), and waves that measure less than 16 Hz are considered infrasound. Our bodies still react to these unhearable sounds, sometimes with confusing consequences.

Infrasound can induce paranoia, fear, panic, or even a change of heart rate or blood pressure. These reactions are probably partially due to evolution and our survival instincts. Infrasound can be created by movement in Earth's crust, which contributes to volcanic eruptions, earthquakes, and tsunamis. So these sounds can signal DANGER to our brains.

The negative reaction to infrasound is especially strong for about one-fifth of the world's population. These people would have severe reactions if they got stuck in a house with certain questionable pipework ...

They might even be forgiven for thinking the house was haunted.

The Shivers

Aside from infrasound, other factors may influence how someone feels in a "haunted house." Some sense a sudden chill in the air, for example. Scientists have investigated this and found scientific explanations for the sudden drop of temperature, such as a nearby drafty chimney or, less obviously, a change in humidity.

In certain parts of a house, the humidity will be higher. On a cold day, when people sense the extra moisture in the air, they feel colder, even though the temperature has not changed.

The opposite effect can happen if it's hot. High humidity actually makes us feel hotter because it stops our sweat from evaporating. So, if a warm house has an area that's *less* humid, when you stand in it you will feel cooler.

Dust to Dust

What about reported sightings of physical ghosts, rather than feelings or sounds? A researcher named Vic Tandy (1955–2005) conducted investigations at the building where he worked, after staff reported seeing dark figures out of the corners of their eyes. Could it have been ghosts?

He looked into it and found that the culprit was an exhaust fan, which was sending out low-frequency vibrations, creating infrasound waves between the walls of the building. The vibration sometimes reacted with people's eyeballs, creating a smeary vision that made them mistake something normal – like a speck of dust passing close to their eyes – for a large, creepy figure.

ALL IN THE MIND

There are other scientific theories for hauntings. Neuroscientist Michael Persinger (1945–2018) did experiments with electromagnetic fields, which push or pull anything that has an electric charge. Persinger engineered a helmet that allowed him to send specific patterns of electromagnetic fields into people's brains.

Subjects of Persinger's experiments reported that, after wearing the helmet for up to half an hour, they sensed an invisible presence in the room. Persinger believed that the electromagnetic fields were interfering with the brain's temporal lobes (which deal with visual memory, emotions, and the understanding of language), making subjects think they were having ghostly experiences.

TOXIC MOLD ...

Another scientist, an American environmental engineer, Professor Shane Rogers, found other explanations for people experiencing ghosts. He found links between "hauntings" and toxic molds in the air, which can bring on irrational fear and dementia.

... AND POISONOUS GAS

One family, who reported supernatural activities in an old house, heard strange noises and sensed the presence of ghosts. They reported being held down in bed, too weak to move. It turned out that there was a problem in the heating system and they were being slowly poisoned by carbon monoxide, which causes hallucinations.

NOT SO SPOOKY

The scary tales of ghosts in haunted houses all seem to have scientific explanations, so you don't need to worry about meeting one anymore. Even if you do meet one, it can't do anything to hurt you because it's probably intangible, remember? Don't let your fear keep you up at night!

Still scared of things that go bump in the night? Of course you aren't.

GHOSTS and HAUNTINGS: EXPLAINED!

GLOSSARY

airborne in the air and flying

antidepressant a drug that is used to treat people suffering from depression

bubonic plague an infectious disease spread by fleas on rats, which killed many people during the Middle Ages

canine teeth pointed teeth near the front of the mouth of humans and other meat-eating animals

carboyhydrate a substance found in foods such as sugar and bread, which provides energy

catalepsy a condition where the muscles of a body go rigid for a period of time

collective weight the total weight when all the amounts in a group are added together

colony a group of birds, insects, or animals that live together

complexion the color of a person's skin, especially the face

condensation to change from a gas to a liquid, for example when water vapor condenses to form small drops of water

decapitation removal of the head

decompose to slowly break down after death

dementia a serious illness of the mind

digestive system the organs inside the body that digest food, including the mouth, stomach, liver, and intestines

disinfect to get rid of microorganisms that are harmful to humans

electromagnetic field an electric and magnetic force field that surrounds a moving electric charge

evaporate to change from a liquid to a gas, for example when liquid water evaporates to form water vapor

gravity the force of attraction that moves things towards the center of Earth or other bodies in space

hallucination the experience of seeing something that is not real because you are ill or have taken a drug

herbal remedies medical treatments made using herbs

immobilize to stop something from moving

immunity the ability to resist disease or harm

infrasound soundwaves measuring less than 16Hz that cannot be heard

intangible invisible and untouchable

microorganism a very small living thing only visible to the human eye with use of a microscope

molecule the smallest amount of a chemical that can exist by itself

mucus membrane skin that produces mucus to prevent it from becoming dry

nervous system all the nerves in your body, together with your brain and spinal cord

nutrition the process of taking in nutrients into an animal or plant

phenomenon something that can be seen to be a fact

pigment a substance that gives something a color

predator an animal that kills and eats other animals

protein a substance found in foods, such as meat, eggs, and milk, which the body needs to grow

rabies an infectious disease of the nervous system that is common in dogs, which makes people and animals go insane

remedy something to cure illness or pain

scalp the skin under the hair on the head

scapegoat someone blamed for something bad that has happened, even though it may not be their fault

shroud a cloth used for wrapping a dead body

supernatural things that are not natural and cannot be explained

superstitious believing in things that are not real or possible

tangible visible and touchable

temporal lobe the part of the brain associated with memory and language

transformation a radical change

translucent able for light to pass through

tuberculosis an infectious disease that affects the lungs

venom poison

viper a family of small, poisonous snakes

FURTHER INFORMATION

FURTHER FREAKY SCIENCE READING:

The Bright and Bold Human Body
by Izzi Howell and Sonya Newland
(Wayland, 2019)
There are books in the series on:
The Digestive System
The Heart, Lungs, and Blood
The Brain and Nervous System
The Reproductive System
The Skeleton and Muscles
The Senses

Cause, Effect, and Chaos in the Human Body
by Paul Mason
(Wayland, 2020)

A Question of Science: Why Don't Your Eyeballs Fall Out? And Other Questions About the Human Body
by Anna Claybourne
(Wayland, 2020)

BOOM Science: Human Body
by Georgia Amson-Bradshaw
(PowerKids Press, 2020)

100% Get the Whole Picture: Human Body
by Paul Mason
(Cavendish Square, 2024)

PLACES TO SEE FREAKY SCIENCE UP CLOSE:

American Museum of Natural History
200 Central Park West
New York, NY 10024
https://www.amnh.org

National Museum of Natural History
10th Street and Constitution Avenue NW
Washington, DC 20560
https:/naturalhistory.si.edu

Natural History Museum
900 Exposition Boulevard
Los Angeles, CA 90007
https://nhm.org

Canada Museum of Nature
240 McLeod Street
Ottawa, ON K2P 2R1
https://nature.ca/en/

INDEX